S0-BAI-240

A2

THINK-A-GRAMS

EVELYNE M. GRAHAM

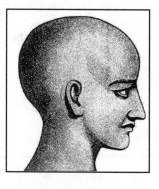

© 1991
THE CRITICAL THINKING CO.
(BRIGHT MINDS™)
www.CriticalThinking.com
P.O. Box 1610 • Seaside • CA 93955-1610
Phone 800-458-4849 • FAX 831-393-3277
ISBN 0-89455-430-1
Reproduction rights granted for single-classroom use only.
Printed in the United States of America

TEACHER SUGGESTIONS AND ANSWERS

SUGGESTIONS

THINK-A-GRAMS are verbal picture puzzles. They can be posted individually, either daily or weekly, on a bulletin board to sharpen students' thinking.

In terms of difficulty, the A level is easiest, B more difficult, and the C level is hardest. Within levels, books 1 and 2 are of similar difficulty.

Each of the books in this series contains an answer key and 100 page-size puzzles. The puzzles provide teachers with an entertaining and challenging tool for coordinating right-brain thinking with left-brain memory. To solve these puzzles, the right brain analyzes the puzzle's symbology and the left brain recalls the common term or phrase depicted.

Since schools devote so much curricula to such left-brain activities as memorization and regurgitation, exposure to more right-brain experiences, such as these THINK-A-GRAMS, helps students develop skills in spatial relations, creative thinking, and problem solving.

Keep in mind that there is frequently more than one answer to a given problem. Encourage students to invent their own THINK-A-GRAMS for your classroom!

ABOUT THE AUTHOR

EVELYNE GRAHAM has 34 years of teaching experience—including all 12 grades—with a major discipline in mathematics. She spent 20 years as Supervisor of Mathematics for Chesapeake Public School System (Virginia), 6 years as Assistant Principal of Instruction at Chesapeake Alternative School, and 10 years as an extension instructor in Mathematics for Elementary Teachers for the University of Virginia.

Mrs. Graham holds an undergraduate degree with triple majors in math, religious education, and music, a masters degree in Mathematics Education, and a Certificate of Advanced Study in School Administration.

Mrs. Graham is a frequent presenter at state and national conferences and the author of books and articles about mathematics education and activities.

ANSWERS A2

1. To overdo
2. Sun spots
3. Head over heels
4. Stand by me
5. Stay on course
6. Screwball
7. Long overdue
8. Bump in the night
9. Set up, upset
10. Cart before the horse
11. Gentle on my mind
12. Downpour
13. Eating between meals
14. Team overmatched
15. Cop on the beat
16. Dashing through the snow
17. Circuits overloaded
18. Flying high, high flying
19. Call on me
20. I'll be over right away
21. Argument between friends
22. All in all
23. Point in time
24. Update
25. Played by ear
26. Depend on it
27. Required by law
28. Singing in the rain
29. Repel
30. Leftover turkey
31. Come on down
32. Putting on weight
33. Saved by the bell
34. One in charge
35. Broken down
36. Are you online?
37. High blood pressure
38. Focus on the target
39. Speak up
40. Taken for granted
41. Jack in the box
42. Open up a can of worms
43. Car overheated
44. High noon
45. Hold up
46. Based on fact
47. Kept under lock and key
48. Just in time
49. Gone for good
50. Thumbs up
51. Pig in a poke
52. Life's overwhelming
53. Just in case
54. High on the hog
55. Always on the move
56. Ten pins
57. Slow down
58. Outgoing or going out
59. Keep in touch
60. Sitting around the house
61. Sidewalk
62. Highbrow
63. A foot in the door
64. Too tired to care
65. Floating on air
66. Your number's up
67. Redefined
68. Turn over a new leaf
69. Singing off key
70. On the job training
71. Lying down on the job
72. Rude and overbearing
73. Upper crust
74. Down draft
75. Vacation overseas
76. Agent undercover
77. Side by side
78. Advocates
79. Lucky break
80. Fingers crossed
81. Hitting below the belt
82. Hibernate
83. Big industry
84. Don't worry about it
85. Countryside
86. Outdated
87. Fly in the ointment
88. Flower in bloom
89. Fall down
90. Taking it in stride
91. Hanging in there
92. Feeling down in the dumps
93. The jig is up
94. Ordered through the mail
95. Double up
96. Crosswalk
97. Weekly reader
98. Feeling down and out
99. Replenish
100. Editor in chief

$$\frac{2}{DO}$$

©1991 Midwest Publications / Critical Thinking Press & Software   P.O. Box 448, Pacific Grove, CA 93950

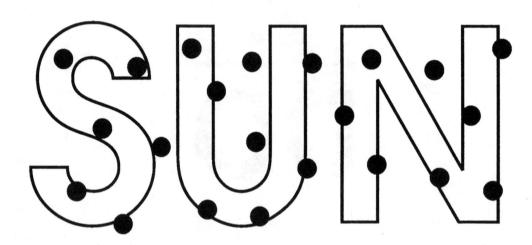

©1991 Midwest Publications / Critical Thinking Press & Software   P.O. Box 448, Pacific Grove, CA 93950

HEAD

HEELS

STAND ME

©1991 Midwest Publications / Critical Thinking Press & Software   P.O. Box 448, Pacific Grove, CA 93950

STAY
COURSE

©1991 Midwest Publications / Critical Thinking Press & Software   P.O. Box 448, Pacific Grove, CA 93950

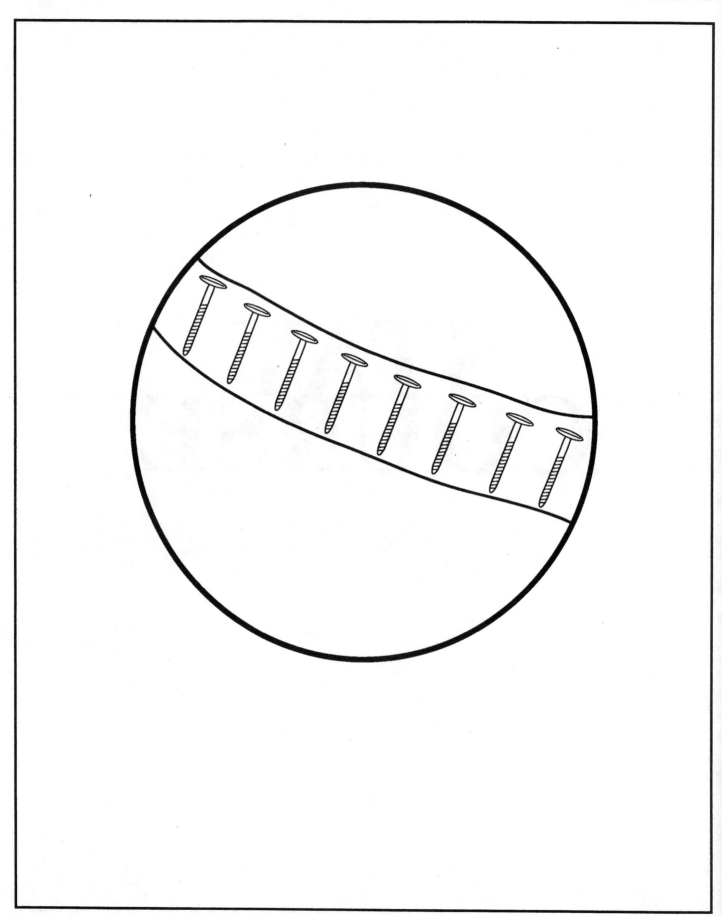

©1991 Midwest Publications / Critical Thinking Press & Software   P.O. Box 448, Pacific Grove, CA 93950

$$\frac{\text{LONG}}{\text{DUE}}$$

NIGBUMPHT

©1991 Midwest Publications / Critical Thinking Press & Software   P.O. Box 448, Pacific Grove, CA 93950

T

E

S

CART   HORSE

©1991 Midwest Publications / Critical Thinking Press & Software P.O. Box 448, Pacific Grove, CA 93950

GENTLE
MY MIND

P
O
U
R

©1991 Midwest Publications / Critical Thinking Press & Software   P.O. Box 448, Pacific Grove, CA 93950

MEALS
EATING
MEALS

$$\frac{\text{TEAM}}{\text{MATCHED}}$$

©1991 Midwest Publications / Critical Thinking Press & Software   P.O. Box 448, Pacific Grove, CA 93950

COP
BEAT

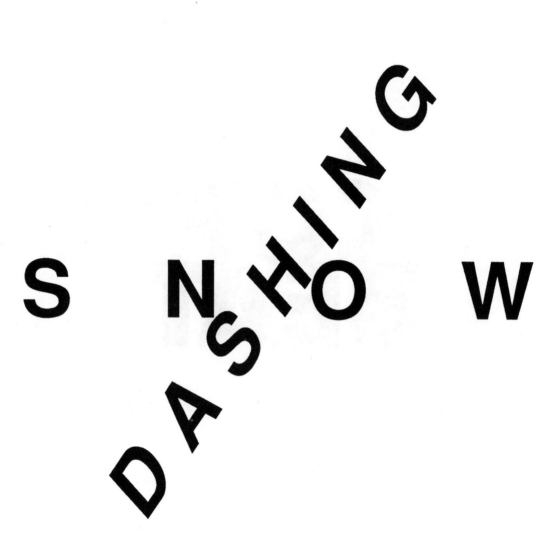

©1991 Midwest Publications / Critical Thinking Press & Software   P.O. Box 448, Pacific Grove, CA 93950

CIRCUITS
——————
LOADED

FLYING

©1991 Midwest Publications / Critical Thinking Press & Software   P.O. Box 448, Pacific Grove, CA 93950

CALL
ME

©1991 Midwest Publications / Critical Thinking Press & Software P.O. Box 448, Pacific Grove, CA 93950

I'LL BE

RIGHT AWAY

©1991 Midwest Publications / Critical Thinking Press & Software   P.O. Box 448, Pacific Grove, CA 93950

FRIENDS
ARGUMENT
FRIENDS

ALALLL

 ©1991 Midwest Publications / Critical Thinking Press & Software   P.O. Box 448, Pacific Grove, CA 93950

TI • ME

©1991 Midwest Publications / Critical Thinking Press & Software   P.O. Box 448, Pacific Grove, CA 93950

E
T
A
D

©1991 Midwest Publications / Critical Thinking Press & Software   P.O. Box 448, Pacific Grove, CA 93950

PLAYED EAR

©1991 Midwest Publications / Critical Thinking Press & Software   P.O. Box 448, Pacific Grove, CA 93950

DEPEND
IT

©1991 Midwest Publications / Critical Thinking Press & Software   P.O. Box 448, Pacific Grove, CA 93950

REQUIRED LAW

RASINGINGIN

©1991 Midwest Publications / Critical Thinking Press & Software   P.O. Box 448, Pacific Grove, CA 93950

PEL

LEFT

TURKEY

©1991 Midwest Publications / Critical Thinking Press & Software   P.O. Box 448, Pacific Grove, CA 93950

PUTTING
WEIGHT

©1991 Midwest Publications / Critical Thinking Press & Software P.O. Box 448, Pacific Grove, CA 93950

~~DING-A-LING~~

~~CHIME~~

SAVED BELL

~~GONG~~

~~BUZZER~~

©1991 Midwest Publications / Critical Thinking Press & Software P.O. Box 448, Pacific Grove, CA 93950

CHA1RGE

©1991 Midwest Publications / Critical Thinking Press & Software P.O. Box 448, Pacific Grove, CA 93950

©1991 Midwest Publications / Critical Thinking Press & Software   P.O. Box 448, Pacific Grove, CA 93950

R U

©1991 Midwest Publications / Critical Thinking Press & Software   P.O. Box 448, Pacific Grove, CA 93950

BLOOD PRESSURE

©1991 Midwest Publications / Critical Thinking Press & Software   P.O. Box 448, Pacific Grove, CA 93950

FOCUS
TARGET

©1991 Midwest Publications / Critical Thinking Press & Software   P.O. Box 448, Pacific Grove, CA 93950

K
A
E
P
S

©1991 Midwest Publications / Critical Thinking Press & Software   P.O. Box 448, Pacific Grove, CA 93950

TAKEN

GRANTED
GRANTED
GRANTED
GRANTED

©1991 Midwest Publications / Critical Thinking Press & Software   P.O. Box 448, Pacific Grove, CA 93950

BJACKOX

©1991 Midwest Publications / Critical Thinking Press & Software   P.O. Box 448, Pacific Grove, CA 93950

N

E

P

O

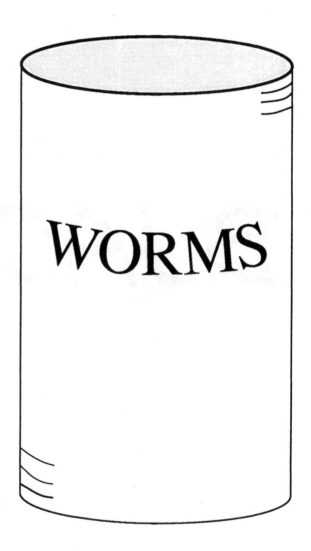

WORMS

©1991 Midwest Publications / Critical Thinking Press & Software   P.O. Box 448, Pacific Grove, CA 93950

NOON

©1991 Midwest Publications / Critical Thinking Press & Software   P.O. Box 448, Pacific Grove, CA 93950

D

L

O

H

©1991 Midwest Publications / Critical Thinking Press & Software   P.O. Box 448, Pacific Grove, CA 93950

BASED
FACT

©1991 Midwest Publications / Critical Thinking Press & Software   P.O. Box 448, Pacific Grove, CA 93950

LOCK AND KEY
KEPT

TIJUSTME

©1991 Midwest Publications / Critical Thinking Press & Software P.O. Box 448, Pacific Grove, CA 93950

GONE

GOOD
GOOD
GOOD
GOOD

S
B
M
U
H
T

©1991 Midwest Publications / Critical Thinking Press & Software   P.O. Box 448, Pacific Grove, CA 93950

POPIGKE

LIFE'S

WHELMING

©1991 Midwest Publications / Critical Thinking Press & Software   P.O. Box 448, Pacific Grove, CA 93950

CAJUSTSE

HIGH
HOG

©1991 Midwest Publications / Critical Thinking Press & Software P.O. Box 448, Pacific Grove, CA 93950

©1991 Midwest Publications / Critical Thinking Press & Software   P.O. Box 448, Pacific Grove, CA 93950

PINS   PINS

PINS   PINS

PINS   PINS

PINS   PINS

PINS   PINS

©1991 Midwest Publications / Critical Thinking Press & Software P.O. Box 448, Pacific Grove, CA 93950

S
L
O
W

©1991 Midwest Publications / Critical Thinking Press & Software   P.O. Box 448, Pacific Grove, CA 93950

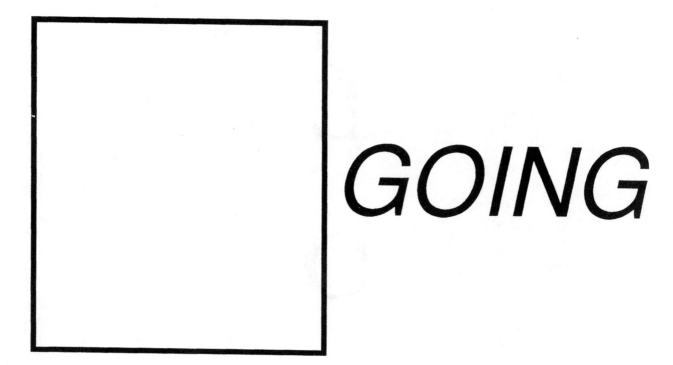

©1991 Midwest Publications / Critical Thinking Press & Software   P.O. Box 448, Pacific Grove, CA 93950

©1991 Midwest Publications / Critical Thinking Press & Software   P.O. Box 448, Pacific Grove, CA 93950

©1991 Midwest Publications / Critical Thinking Press & Software   P.O. Box 448, Pacific Grove, CA 93950

WALK

©1991 Midwest Publications / Critical Thinking Press & Software   P.O. Box 448, Pacific Grove, CA 93950

DOFOOTOR

TIRED
TIRED

CARE
CARE

©1991 Midwest Publications / Critical Thinking Press & Software   P.O. Box 448, Pacific Grove, CA 93950

FLOATING
AIR

©1991 Midwest Publications / Critical Thinking Press & Software   P.O. Box 448, Pacific Grove, CA 93950

S
R
E
B
M
U
N
R
U
O
Y

©1991 Midwest Publications / Critical Thinking Press & Software   P.O. Box 448, Pacific Grove, CA 93950

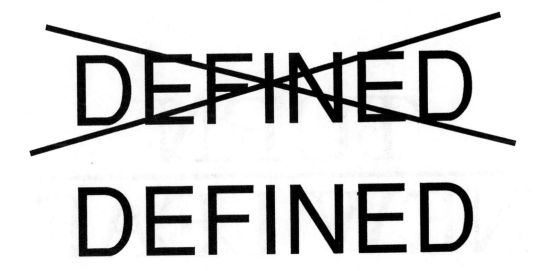

©1991 Midwest Publications / Critical Thinking Press & Software P.O. Box 448, Pacific Grove, CA 93950

TURN

NEW LEAF

©1991 Midwest Publications / Critical Thinking Press & Software   P.O. Box 448, Pacific Grove, CA 93950

SINGING
KEY

KEY SINGING

TRAINING
JOB

©1991 Midwest Publications / Critical Thinking Press & Software P.O. Box 448, Pacific Grove, CA 93950

L
Y
I
N
G
JOB

RUDE AND
─────────────
BEARING

©1991 Midwest Publications / Critical Thinking Press & Software P.O. Box 448, Pacific Grove, CA 93950

CRUST

CRUST

D
R
A
F
T

©1991 Midwest Publications / Critical Thinking Press & Software   P.O. Box 448, Pacific Grove, CA 93950

VACATION

SEAS

COVER

AGENT

©1991 Midwest Publications / Critical Thinking Press & Software P.O. Box 448, Pacific Grove, CA 93950

SIDE SIDE

vocates
+ vocates

©1991 Midwest Publications / Critical Thinking Press & Software P.O. Box 448, Pacific Grove, CA 93950

F I N G E R S

F I N G E R S

©1991 Midwest Publications / Critical Thinking Press & Software P.O. Box 448, Pacific Grove, CA 93950

BELT

HITTING

BERNATE

©1991 Midwest Publications / Critical Thinking Press & Software   P.O. Box 448, Pacific Grove, CA 93950

DUSBIGTRY

©1991 Midwest Publications / Critical Thinking Press & Software   P.O. Box 448, Pacific Grove, CA 93950

COUNTRY

DATED

 ©1991 Midwest Publications / Critical Thinking Press & Software P.O. Box 448, Pacific Grove, CA 93950

OIFLYNTMENT

BLOFLOWEROM

©1991 Midwest Publications / Critical Thinking Press & Software   P.O. Box 448, Pacific Grove, CA 93950

FALL

STRTAKINGITIDE

©1991 Midwest Publications / Critical Thinking Press & Software   P.O. Box 448, Pacific Grove, CA 93950

THEHANGINGRE

F
E
E
D U L M P S
I
N
G

©1991 Midwest Publications / Critical Thinking Press & Software P.O. Box 448, Pacific Grove, CA 93950

S
I
G
I
J
E
H
T

©1991 Midwest Publications / Critical Thinking Press & Software   P.O. Box 448, Pacific Grove, CA 93950

©1991 Midwest Publications / Critical Thinking Press & Software   P.O. Box 448, Pacific Grove, CA 93950

UP
UP

©1991 Midwest Publications / Critical Thinking Press & Software   P.O. Box 448, Pacific Grove, CA 93950

W
WALK
L
K

©1991 Midwest Publications / Critical Thinking Press & Software   P.O. Box 448, Pacific Grove, CA 93950

KLY **READER**

```
F
E
E
L
I
N
G
```

AND

©1991 Midwest Publications / Critical Thinking Press & Software   P.O. Box 448, Pacific Grove, CA 93950

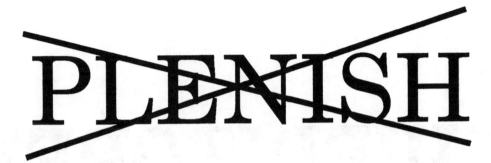

PLENISH

CHIEDITOREF

©1991 Midwest Publications / Critical Thinking Press & Software   P.O. Box 448, Pacific Grove, CA 93950